I ♥ SCOTLAND
Colouring

Illustrated by John MacGregor

HOMETOWN WORLD

First published by HOMETOWN WORLD in 2011
Hometown World Ltd, 7 Northumberland Buildings, Bath BA1 2JB
www.hometownworld.co.uk
Copyright © Hometown World Ltd 2011

ISBN 978-1-84993-228-8
Printed in China

Highland Games!

Draw over the dotted lines to finish the Scottish piper's hat and bagpipes. Then colour him in.

Fun Fact
The Highland Games include throwing the hammer, tossing the caber, putting the shot, tug o' war, racing, dancing and piping competitions.

Isle of Skye!

Add two more paddles to help the canoe on its way.

Fun Fact
Vikings once lived on the Isle of Skye in the Hebrides.

Try!

Draw over the dotted lines to finish the Scottish flag. Then colour it blue and white.

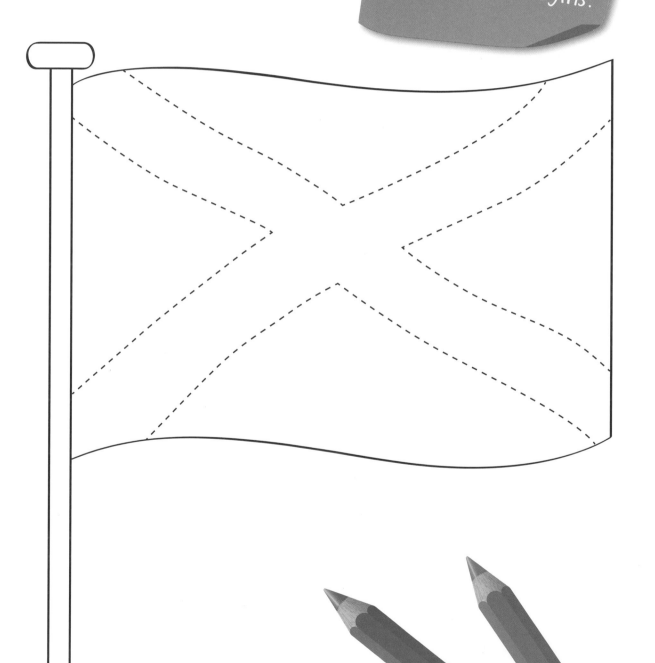

Go Wild!

Add an antler to each deer to finish the picture. Then colour them in.

Edinburgh Zoo

Draw a fish to feed the hungry penguins at Edinburgh Zoo.

Fun Fact
Edinburgh Castle, in Scotland's capital city, is built on an ancient volcano!

Royal Visit

Add a golf ball next to the hole to win the match. Then colour in the picture.

Fun Fact
People have played golf at the Royal and Ancient Golf Club of St Andrews for over 250 years.

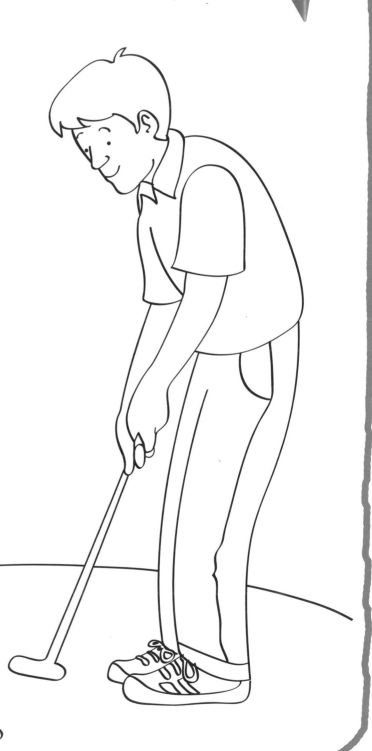

Visit the RRS **Discovery** at **Dundee** and find out about **Scott's** journey to the **Antarctic**.

Bike Trail!

Draw the spokes on the bike wheels.
Then colour in the picture.

Goal!

Colour in your team's football strip and add a number.

Fun Fact
You can see the Scottish Cup at the Scottish Football Museum, Hampden Park, in Glasgow.

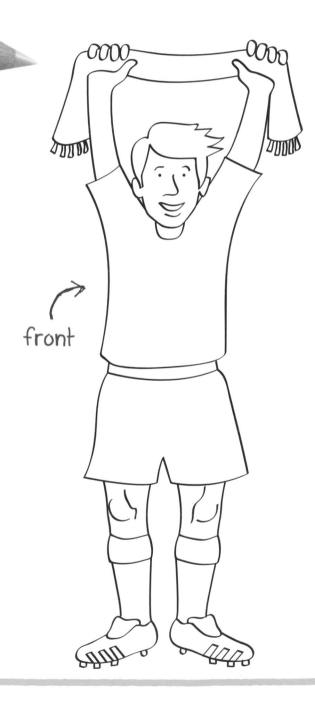

front

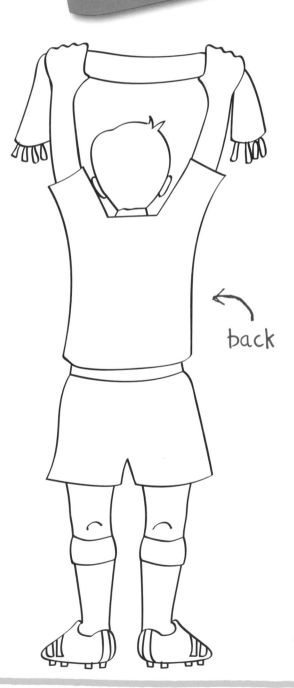

back

Monster in the Loch!

Draw over the dotted lines to finish the Loch Ness Monster. Then colour in the picture.

Fun Fact
St Columba spotted the Loch Ness Monster over 1,400 years ago!

Loch Lomond

Draw a sail on the boat. Then colour it in.

Fun Fact
Loch Lomond is the largest freshwater lake in Britain.

Flying High

Draw a colourful pattern on the kite. Add bows to the tail.

Big Catch!

There are plenty of salmon in the River Tweed. Draw a fish on the end of his line. Then colour the picture.

Fun Fact
Sir Walter Scott who wrote 'Rob Roy' lived in Abbotsford, near Melrose.

Picture Perfect

Draw a picture of yourself.
Then decorate the picture frame.

John O'Groats

Add the name of your home town to the sign. Then colour in the picture.

JOHN O'GROATS

LANDS END 874

PENTLAND SKERRIES 6

ORKNEY & SHETLAND ISLES

Fun at the Fair

Add poles to join the horses to the merry-go-round. Then colour it in.

Whizz! Bang!

Colour in the fireworks.

Braw!

Wow!

Colourful **fireworks light up** the **sky** for **Hogmanay.**